Eli Learns to Beware

Don't Throw Trash on the Ground;
There are People Around!

Written by: R. Gold

Illustrations: Nechama Leibler

Translation and Rhymes by: Shoshana Lepon

Designed by: Rachel Yagelnik

goldbsd@gmail.com | goldbsd.co.il

During recess Eli sees a banana peel
right where his friends go to play.
He runs over to pick it up
and throws it out, right away.

Eli's friends watch him
clean up the trash.
"Why are you cleaning
the playground?" they ask.
"Why are you picking up yucky stuff?
We throw out our own garbage;
isn't that enough?"

Eli tells them,
"My Grandpa is an old man
but he still goes shopping
for Shabbat when he can.
I go with him to help him
and together we choose
the nicest fruits and vegetables
without a bump or bruise.

Last month the worker
sat down to eat
and threw a peel
on the ground by his feet.

4.20

6.00

My grandpa walked past
and stepped with his heel
on the mushy, slippery banana peel.
He went sliding and then fell down.
He got hurt when he hit the ground.

"That's awful!" all the boys say.
"What happened to your grandpa
that day?"
"My grandpa broke both of his legs.
Hatzalah came to help him right away.
They took him in the ambulance
to the hospital for a stay."

"In the hospital the doctor said,
'You're lucky you didn't fall
on your head!'
When I went to visit him
he gave me a talk,
'Be careful not to throw things
where people walk!'"

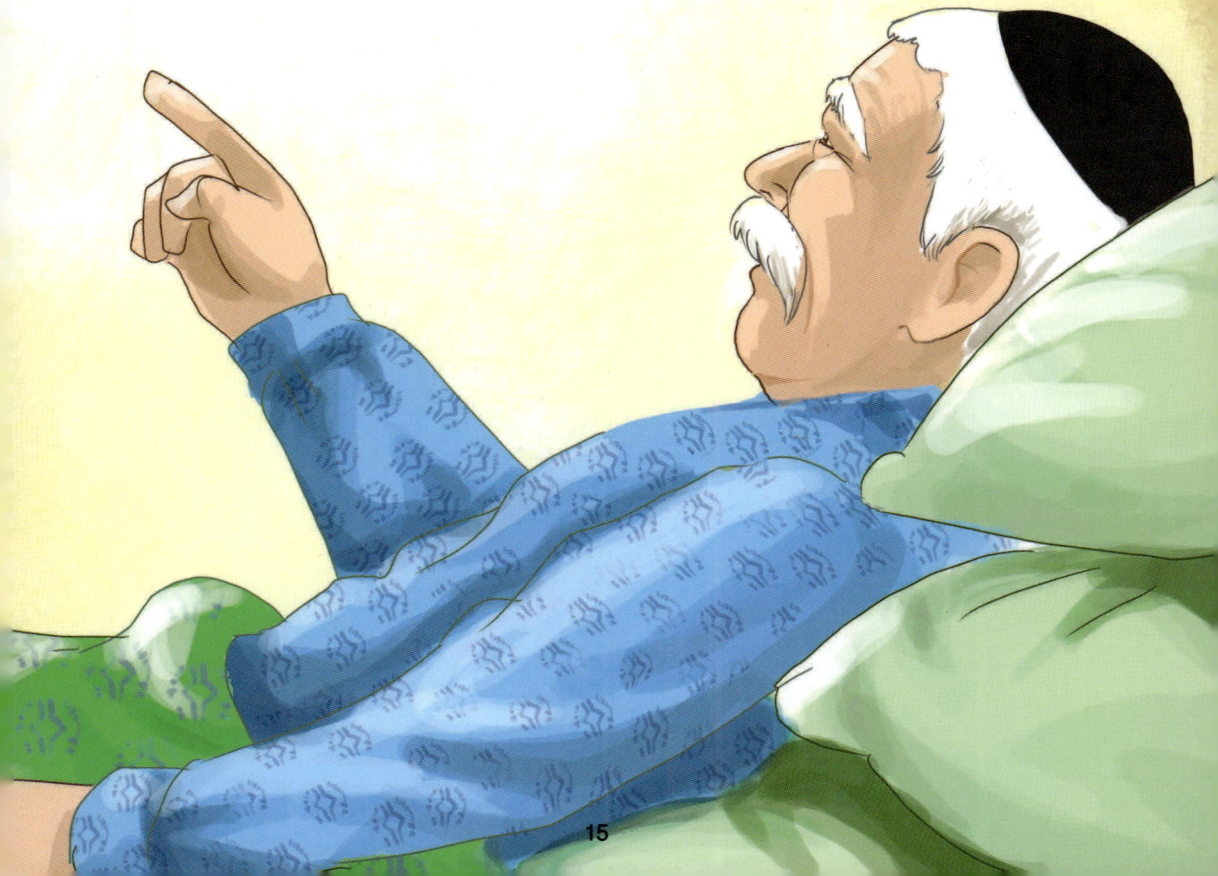

"My grandpa's in a wheelchair;
his legs are in a cast.
We pray that he'll get better
and be walking again real fast.
So you see how dangerous
it is to drop
things where people may
not see and stop."

Eli and all his friends now know:
peels and bags and wrappers…
into the trash they go!